THE
Fantastic
CUTAWAY BOOK OF
GIANT
BUILDINGS

JON KIRKWOOD *AND* ALEX PANG

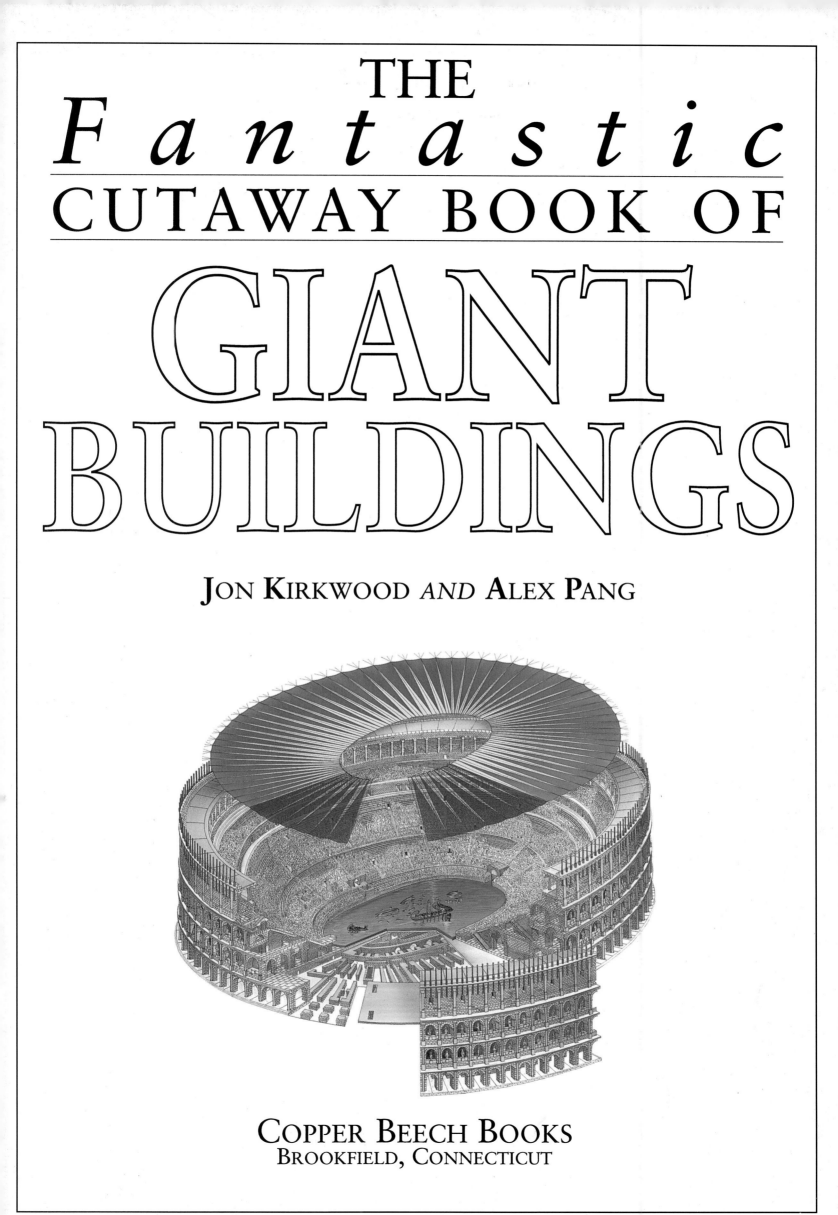

COPPER BEECH BOOKS
BROOKFIELD, CONNECTICUT

*First published in the
United States in 1997 by
Copper Beech Books
an imprint of
The Millbrook Press
2 Old New Milford Road
Brookfield, Connecticut
06804*

Printed in Belgium

Editor
Jon Richards
Design
David West
Children's Book Design
Designer
Robert Perry
Picture research
Brooks Krikler Research
Illustrators Alex Pang and
Mike Saunders

5 4 3 2 1

**Library of Congress
Cataloging-in-Publication Data**
Kirkwood, Jon.
The fantastic cutaway book of
giant buildings /
Jon Kirkwood ;
illustrated by Alex Pang
p. cm.
Includes index.
Summary: Cross-section
illustrations invite the reader to
peer inside cathedrals, castles
and palaces, industrial giants,
and other buildings to see how
they were built.
ISBN 0-7613-0615-3 (lib. bdg.).
— ISBN 0-7613-0629-3 (pbk.)
1. Tall buildings—Juvenile
literature. 2. Historic buildings—
Juvenile literature.
3. Commercial buildings—
Juvenile literature. [1. Tall
buildings. 2. Historic buildings.
3. Commercial buildings.]
I. Pang, Alex, ill. II. Title.
TH143.H48 1997   97 1008
720.'483—dc21   CIP AC

CONTENTS

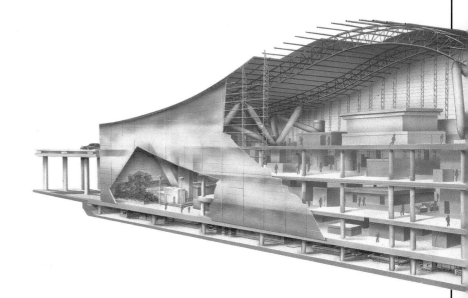

INTRODUCTION

Since the earliest days of human civilization, people have constructed large and impressive buildings. These huge structures have fulfilled a wide range of roles, from places in which to live and work, to massive power stations, places of worship, and even monuments.

From the end of the 19th century, when the first skyscrapers were built, improvements in building materials and design have led to the construction of ever-bigger structures. Today, huge office buildings stretch into the sky for hundreds of feet.

The future holds many challenges for tomorrow's builders. With the population of the world increasing and the planet having only a limited amount of land to build on, new answers need to be found to cope with the shortage of space. Solutions range from the practical to the bizarre. They include cities in the sky, deep beneath the ground, or even in space!

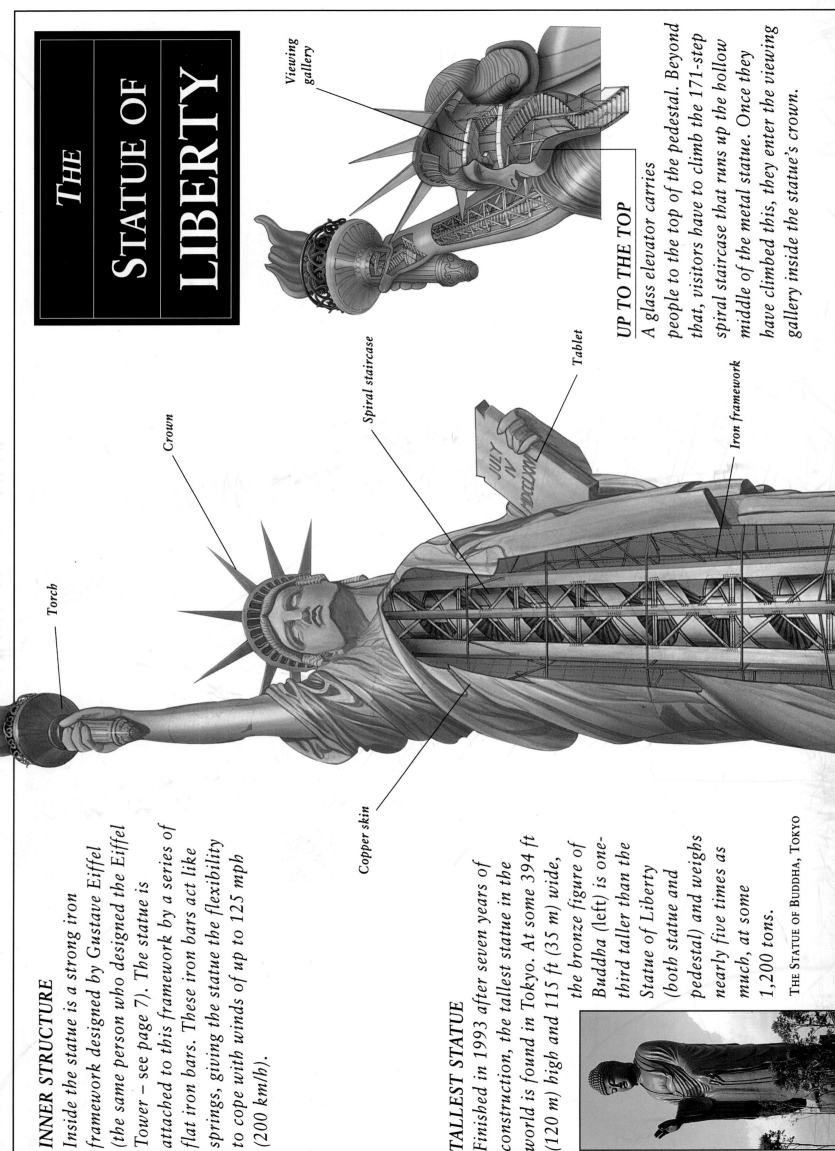

THE STATUE OF LIBERTY

Viewing gallery

UP TO THE TOP

A glass elevator carries people to the top of the pedestal. Beyond that, visitors have to climb the 171-step spiral staircase that runs up the hollow middle of the metal statue. Once they have climbed this, they enter the viewing gallery inside the statue's crown.

Tablet

Iron framework

Crown

Spiral staircase

Torch

Copper skin

INNER STRUCTURE

Inside the statue is a strong iron framework designed by Gustave Eiffel (the same person who designed the Eiffel Tower – see page 7). The statue is attached to this framework by a series of flat iron bars. These iron bars act like springs, giving the statue the flexibility to cope with winds of up to 125 mph (200 km/h).

TALLEST STATUE

Finished in 1993 after seven years of construction, the tallest statue in the world is found in Tokyo. At some 394 ft (120 m) high and 115 ft (35 m) wide, the bronze figure of Buddha (left) is one-third taller than the Statue of Liberty (both statue and pedestal) and weighs nearly five times as much, at some 1,200 tons.

THE STATUE OF BUDDHA, TOKYO

DIMENSIONS

The crown of the statue is 302 ft (92 m) above the ground. The metal statue, at 154 ft (46 m) tall, makes up half of this height, while the remainder is made up by the stone pedestal. Together, the copper statue and its iron framework weigh 220 tons. However, the copper skin weighs only 32.5 tons because the metal exterior is relatively thin.

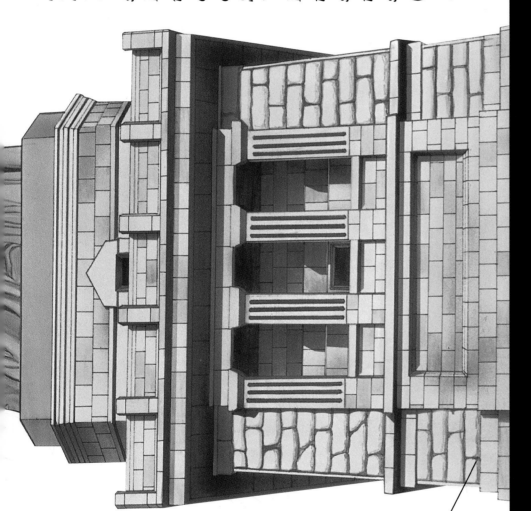

Stone pedestal

THE MOTHERLAND

The massive statue of the "Motherland" (right), situated on Mamayev Hill, outside Volgograd, was built to commemorate the defense of the city (then called Stalingrad) during World War II (1939–1945). From its base to the tip of the sword carried in the figure's right hand, the statue measures 270 ft (82 m) high.

THE MOTHERLAND, VOLGOGRAD

HIGH ABOVE the entrance to New York Harbor stands one of the most famous statues in the world – the Statue of Liberty. The enormous statue of a woman holding the torch of freedom in her right hand was a gift from the French people to the United States, celebrating the strong relationship between the two countries.

Designed by the French sculptor Frédéric Auguste Bartholdi, the statue was built in Paris over a period of fifteen years, between 1870 and 1885. It was then broken up and put into 210 crates and shipped across the Atlantic to America. When it arrived the statue was put together again on top of a stone pedestal on a small island, where it stands today.

STATUE OF LIBERTY

MONUMENTS OF THE WORLD

PYRAMIDS OF THE SUN AND MOON

TEOTIHUACÁN

The Egyptians were not the only people to build pyramids. Central American civilizations also built them to use as temples. The best known of these are the Pyramid of the Sun and the Pyramid of the Moon (above) in the city of Teotihuacán near modern-day Mexico City. The huge Pyramid of the Moon lies at the north end of the city, but is dwarfed by the great Pyramid of the Sun. This enormous temple is 720 by 760 ft (220 m by 230 m) along its rectangular base and reaches a height of 216 ft (66 m).

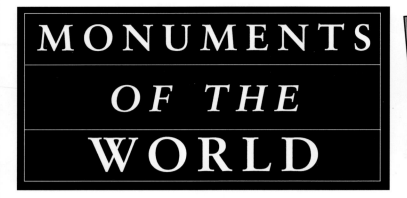

THE PYRAMID OF CHEOPS, GIZA

Capstone

King's burial chamber

Great gallery

Second burial chamber

First burial chamber

Limestone covering

THE COLOSSUS OF RHODES

OTHER WONDERS

The Pyramids at Giza are the only surviving remains of the Seven Wonders of the Ancient World. The other wonders were: the Hanging Gardens of Babylon; the Temple of Artemis at Ephesus; the Statue of Zeus at Olympia; the Pharos of Alexandria, a lighthouse on the island of Pharos off Alexandria; the Mausoleum of Halicarnassus, the huge tomb of Mausolus (left), the ruler of Caria in southwestern Asia Minor; and the Colossus of Rhodes, a mighty bronze statue that stood 100 ft (30 m) above the Harbor of Rhodes (above).

THE TOMB OF MAUSOLUS

S ome of the most impressive buildings in the world serve no practical purpose. Instead they stand as monuments, celebrating the achievements of individuals or, like the Statue of Liberty, the friendship between two countries (see page 4).

Among the oldest and perhaps the greatest monuments still standing are the pyramids at Giza in Egypt. These three pyramids were built as tombs for three of the ancient Egyptian rulers. The largest, the Pyramid of Cheops (above), built between 2660 and 2560 B.C., contains over two million blocks of stone, each with an average weight of 2.5 tons. It has a square base, with each side being 755 ft (230 m) long and is 451 ft (138 m) high. Inside are several tunnels, galleries, and chambers designed to contain and hide the king's burial place.

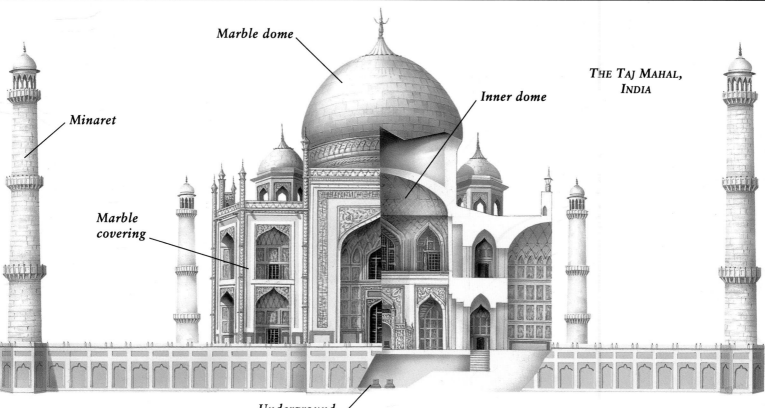

Marble dome

Inner dome

THE TAJ MAHAL, INDIA

Minaret

Marble covering

Underground tombs

THE TAJ MAHAL

The Taj Mahal (above) near Agra, India, was built by the Mogul Emperor Shah Jahan as a tomb for his wife Mumtaz Mahal, who died during childbirth in 1631. Building started in the following year and was finished in 1654. The dome of the Taj Mahal stands 250 ft (76 m) high, and the exterior of the building is decorated with crystal and lapis lazuli, a semi-precious stone.

PARIS MONUMENTS

Paris contains many monuments celebrating its history. The Eiffel Tower (right) is an iron structure, 1,050 ft (320 m) high, designed by Gustave Eiffel for the Centennial Exposition of 1889 commemorating the French Revolution of 1789. One of the most striking buildings of the city is La Grande Arche in La Défense (left). This massive square arch is big enough to contain Notre Dame Cathedral (see page 8). It holds an exhibition hall and a conference center.

LA GRANDE ARCHE

THE EIFFEL TOWER

ST. LOUIS ARCH

The Gateway to the West (below), in St. Louis, is a stainless-steel arch that is 630 ft (192 m) high and wide. It was built to celebrate the historic role of St. Louis as the "Gateway to the West," after the expansion of the United States with the Louisiana Purchase of 1803. This purchase of land from France doubled the size of the United States.

THE GATEWAY TO THE WEST, ST. LOUIS

ST. PAUL'S CATHEDRAL BY NIGHT

PLACES OF WORSHIP have always been impressive buildings, reflecting the grandeur of the age they were built in. One of the great buildings of the late 17th century is St. Paul's Cathedral. Following the destruction of the old St. Paul's Cathedral in the Great Fire of London in 1666, the architect Sir Christopher Wren was charged with building its successor. Construction of his new, domed cathedral began in 1675 and continued for another 35 years. It was finally completed in 1710. Since then, St. Paul's Cathedral has survived many changes that have occurred to the city of London and even the Blitz of World War II.

NOTRE DAME

Situated on the Île de la Cité, a small island in the middle of the Seine River in Paris, is Notre Dame Cathedral (right). It was built between 1163 and 1250 and was one of the first buildings to use arched supports, called flying buttresses. During the French Revolution of 1789, it was damaged and was not restored until 1864.

NOTRE DAME, PARIS

Northwest tower

ST. PAUL'S CATHEDRAL

West entrance

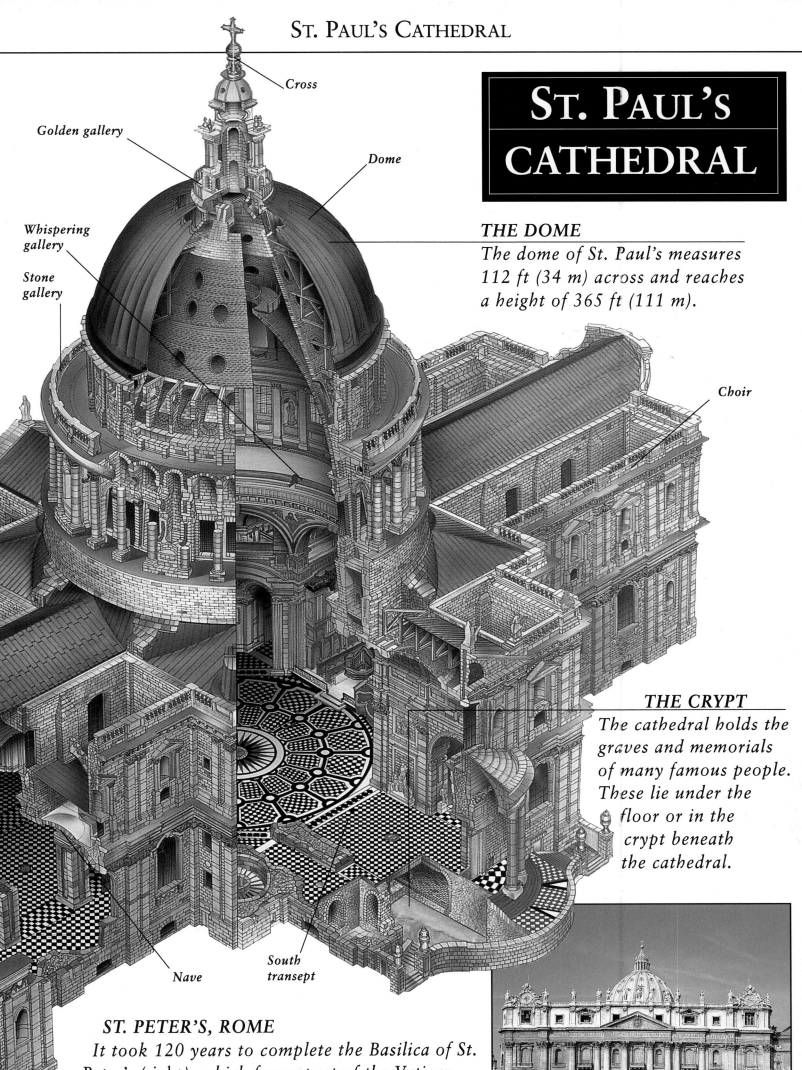

Cross

Golden gallery

Dome

Whispering gallery

Stone gallery

Choir

Nave

South transept

St. Paul's CATHEDRAL

THE DOME
The dome of St. Paul's measures 112 ft (34 m) across and reaches a height of 365 ft (111 m).

THE CRYPT
The cathedral holds the graves and memorials of many famous people. These lie under the floor or in the crypt beneath the cathedral.

ST. PETER'S, ROME
It took 120 years to complete the Basilica of St. Peter's (right), which forms part of the Vatican City in Rome. The foundations were laid in 1506, and the church was finished in 1626. On top of the cathedral, which is 690 ft (210 m) long, is a massive dome designed by the artist and architect Michelangelo. The dome is 400 ft (120 m) high.

ST. PETER'S, ROME

CHURCHES AND TEMPLES

MECCA

The religion of Islam requires all of its followers to make a pilgrimage, or hajj, to the Great Mosque at Mecca in Saudi Arabia (below right). This enormous building is visited by some two million pilgrims during Dhu alhijja, the last month of the Muslim year. At the center of the mosque's courtyard sits the Ka'aba, or "square house." Found within this is a sacred black stone that is said to have fallen from heaven into the Garden of Eden.

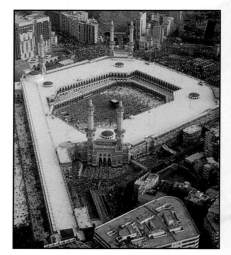

THE GREAT MOSQUE, MECCA

TEMPLE OF RAMESES II, ABU SIMBEL

Since the dawn of civilization, people have built massive churches or temples. As early as 1250 B.C., the Egyptian ruler, Rameses II, built a temple at Abu Simbel. The front of this is guarded by four figures of Rameses, each over 66 ft (20 m) high (above). The Temple of Karnak (right) covers 215,000 sq ft (20,000 sq m) near Luxor in southern Egypt.

HALL OF PILLARS, KARNAK

ANGKOR WAT

Built between the 9th and 13th centuries, the now deserted city of Angkor in Cambodia covers an area stretching 15 miles (24 km) from west to east and 5 miles (8 km) from north to south. The best preserved of its temples is Angkor Wat (below). Constructed between A.D. 1113 and 1150, Angkor Wat covers an area of 1 sq mile (2.5 sq km), making it one of the largest religious complexes ever built.

ANGKOR WAT

THE PARTHENON

Standing high above Athens, Greece, on top of the Acropolis (meaning "high city"), is the Parthenon (right). This temple was built between 447 and 432 B.C. and dedicated to the patron goddess of Athens, Athena. Standing 60 ft (18 m) high, it is 240 ft (72 m) long and 110 ft (34 m) wide and is supported by 46 marble columns. Inside the temple stood a huge statue of Athena that was decorated with over a ton of gold!

Sculptures showing the life of the goddess Athena

THE PARTHENON, ATHENS

Statue of Athena

Inner chamber

Marble column

HAGIA SOPHIA

In A.D. 532, the Byzantine Emperor Justinian began construction of the massive church of Hagia Sophia in Constantinople (now called Istanbul). A huge team of 10,000 workers took just five years to complete the building of the domed church (left). In the 15th century the church was turned into a mosque. Today, Hagia Sophia is a museum.

HAGIA SOPHIA, ISTANBUL

SAGRADA FAMILIA, BARCELONA

MODERN CATHEDRALS

The largest church in the world is the modern Basilica of Our Lady of Peace in the Côte d'Ivoire, Africa (below). The dome is 519 ft (158 m) high and the church can seat nearly 7,000 people. Another modern cathedral is the church of the Sagrada Familia ("Holy Family") in Barcelona (right). Designed by the Spanish architect Antonio Gaudi, this ornate church was started in 1882 and is still unfinished.

BASILICA OF OUR LADY OF PEACE

MEDIEVAL CASTLE

TOWER POWER

Castle towers fulfilled a number of different roles in the defense of a fortress. They were built to deflect missiles from catapults and could act as both lookout places and as strong points in walls from where defenders could shoot missiles at the attackers below them.

FOOD AND WATER

Beneath many castles lay huge cellars that were filled with supplies for use in the event of a siege. A castle also needed its own water supply. Some, such as Krak des Chevaliers, had an aqueduct and a reservoir between the inner and outer walls. This reservior also acted as a water-filled ditch to make taking the castle even more

Central keep

Tower

Store rooms

THE TOWER OF LONDON

TOWER OF LONDON
Work started on the Tower of London (left) in 1066 soon after the crowning of William the Conqueror. The stone central keep, the 90-ft (27-m) high White Tower, was started in 1078. It was finished in 1091 and has not changed much in nine centuries.

RINGS OF STONE
Castles often had several sets of surrounding walls. If an attacker broke through one set of walls, the defenders could still hold out and mount a counterattack from within the inner walls. Castle walls could be up to 30 ft (9 m) thick.

GUARDING THE GATE
The gatehouse was always the most vulnerable site in the castle because it was an opening in the walls. In many castles this part of the wall was very heavily fortified to protect this weak spot.

Drawbridge

Moat

BEFORE ARTILLERY was invented, castles played a key role as strongholds against enemy armies. Thousands of these castles were built in medieval Europe and the Middle East until the end of the 16th century. Many still stand, including Krak des Chevaliers ("Castle of the Knights") in Syria (*below*) and the Tower of London. After the arrival of cannons that could destroy castle walls, the role of these heavily fortified buildings changed. More modern fortified buildings bear little resemblance to medieval castles. For example, the Maginot line, a huge chain of fortresses built by the French before World War II, was almost entirely underground.

KRAK DES CHEVALIERS, SYRIA

CASTLES AND PALACES

THE ALHAMBRA PALACE

Most of this palace and fortress of the Moorish rulers of Granada in Spain was built between A.D. 1248 and 1354. The forbidding exterior hides an oasis of gardens and courts containing fountains and pools. Parts of the Alhambra are decorated with beautiful glazed wall tiles that are covered in ornate patterns. The Court of Lions in the center of the castle (right) has some 100 columns, and the colonnade they support provides shade from the heat of the sun.

THE ALHAMBRA PALACE

EDINBURGH CASTLE

Built to reflect the importance of their role, castles and palaces have always been imposing places, dominating their immediate surroundings. Set on the craggy outcrop of Castle Rock, Edinburgh Castle (above) towers over the heart of Scotland's capital city. Its location, which is 443 ft (134 m) above sea level, gives it natural protection on three sides, while the fourth side is very heavily fortified.

FANTASY CASTLE

Neuschwanstein Castle (below) is perched on top of a rock ledge that overlooks the Pöllat Gorge in the Bavarian Alps, Germany. This elaborate building was started in 1869 on the instructions of Bavaria's King Ludwig II, known as "Mad Ludwig." Based on his ideas of what a medieval castle should look like, the castle was a fantasy home for the King. It has soaring spires, towers and turrets, battlements, a walled courtyard, an indoor garden, and even an artificial cave.

NEUSCHWANSTEIN

VERSAILLES

VERSAILLES

The Palace of Versailles (above) was one of the French royal palaces built around Paris. It included about 11 million sq ft (1 million sq m) of gardens. The most impressive room is the Hall of Mirrors. This is 235 ft (72 m) long, and was used for public occasions. Versailles was also a seat of government, housing 1,000 courtiers and 4,000 attendants.

HIMEJI CASTLE

Built in the 14th century as a fortress for the local warlord, Himeji Castle (above) is a strongpoint on the Harima Plain in Japan. The central white multi-story keep, or tenshu, is protected by outer fortifications and has its own formidable sloped walls. Built when guns were just starting to be used, the castle has special narrow openings, or gunports, so the castle defenders could fire on enemy troops attacking the fortress.

THE RED FORT

The aptly named Red Fort (below), also known as Lal Qal'ah, was built by the Mogul emperors in Old Delhi, India. Its construction was started by Shah Jahan, who ruled between 1628 and 1658, and who was also responsible for the building of the Taj Mahal (see page 7). The red sandstone walls of the fort contained several ornate gardens and many fine buildings, including palaces and barracks.

THE RED FORT, DELHI

FORBIDDEN CITY

The sprawling complex of buildings that is the Forbidden City (below left) in Beijing, was home to the emperors of China from 1421 to 1911. It is called "forbidden" because no one without business with the Imperial family was allowed in. Surrounding it is a wall that is 35 ft (11 m) high and 10 miles (16 km) long.

The biggest of the 1,000 buildings in the Forbidden City is the Hall of Supreme Harmony (below). This is a wooden-framed building some 115 ft (35 m) high. The roof is supported by 20 wooden columns, and the whole building stands on a platform made of marble. Inside the Hall is the throne once used by the Emperor.

The Hall of
Supreme Harmony

PLAN OF THE
FORBIDDEN CITY

Emperor's
throne

THE HALL OF
SUPREME HARMONY

THE COLOSSEUM, ROME

CONSTRUCTION OF THE massive oval-shaped bowl of the Colosseum in Rome was started about A.D. 70, during the reign of the Emperor Vespasian. Built of concrete and limestone, it took about ten years to build and played host to a variety of "games." These included gladiator combat (called venation), as well as fights between animals and men, mini-battles, and even sea battles where the arena was flooded and small ships were sailed in it.

The Colosseum could hold more than 50,000 spectators, making it the largest amphitheater in the Roman Empire. It was used until the 5th or 6th centuries when the last gladiator contests were held there.

DIMENSIONS

The Colosseum (right) is 160 ft (48 m) high, 615 ft (190 m) long, and 470 ft (155 m) wide. The arena measures 300 ft (85 m) by 170 ft (55 m). Around this stands a wall, which is 15 ft (4.5 m) high, that separated the crowd from the action.

Supporting poles

UNDER THE ARENA

Below the arena of the Colosseum was a complicated maze of tunnels, cells, and rooms. This area was where animals were kept and where gladiators or prisoners waited before going to fight. Special trapdoors and elevators carried the gladiators and animals up to the arena floor.

Velarium

Third tier
of seats

Second tier
of seats

First tier
of seats

Arena

Statue

THE COLOSSEUM

AGAINST THE ELEMENTS

To keep the spectators sheltered from the weather, a huge canvas canopy, called a velarium, could be set up over the Colosseum. It was supported by 240 poles which stood above the upper level. The velarium was set up by sailors from the Roman naval base at nearby Ostia.

ROMAN AMPHITHEATERS

The remains of about 75 amphitheaters have been found throughout what was the Roman Empire. They measure between 200 to 300 ft (60 to 90 m) long and 115 to 200 ft (35 to 60 m) wide. One of the most impressive of these is found at the Roman colony of Thysdrus (now called El Djem) in Tunisia (below).

THE COLOSSEUM AT EL DJEM

CENTERS OF ENTERTAINMENT

CRYSTAL PALACE

THE CRYSTAL PALACE

Built to house the Great Exhibition of 1851, the Crystal Palace (right) was a huge building of glass and iron. It was 1,848 ft (563 m) long, 408 ft (124 m) wide, and 108 ft (33 m) high. The building covered a huge 968,000 sq ft (90,000 sq m) – enough to hold 18 soccer fields. Once the exhibition had finished, the Crystal Palace was taken down and then rebuilt in south London between 1852 and 1854. Unfortunately, it was destroyed by a fire on November 30, 1936.

GREEK AMPHITHEATER

Some of the earliest people to construct buildings for entertainment were the ancient Greeks who built many amphitheaters (above) throughout the Mediterranean. The audience sat in the auditorium, a semicircular bank of benches and seats made of wood or stone, that was usually cut into the side of a hill. Because of the steep slope everyone had a good view of the action, and the shape also helped the sound carry to all parts of the theater. The great theater in Athens, built about 500 B.C., could hold up to 30,000 people.

MAYAN BALL COURT

A ritual game that took place in special ball courts, called tlachtlis, was played by the civilizations of Central America from about 800 B.C. until A.D. 1500. The game, called pok-ta-pok by the Mayans and ollama by the Aztecs, was played in a court shaped like a capital letter "I." Players used their elbows, knees, and hips (but not hands) to send a rubber ball into their opponent's end of the court. In a later variation of the game, the ball had to be hit through several stone rings on either side of the court. The game was very rough and players were often severely injured or even killed.

Stone rings

Arena   MAYAN BALL COURT

Terraces

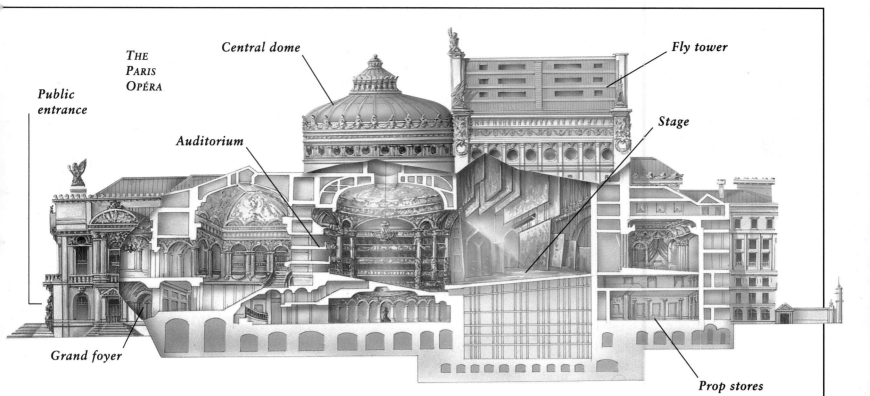

Public entrance

THE PARIS OPÉRA

Central dome

Auditorium

Fly tower

Stage

Grand foyer

Prop stores

OPERA HOUSES

Designed by Charles Garnier, the Paris Opéra (above) was opened on January 5, 1875. The theater holds 2,000 people in its auditorium and can accommodate about 450 performers on the stage. Another opera house, and one of the most striking buildings of the 20th century, is the Sydney Opera House (right). The building's shell-like roofs hold four halls, including the 1,547-seater opera hall and the bigger 2,679-seater concert hall.

OLYMPIC STADIUM, MUNICH

THE OPERA HOUSE, SYDNEY

THE OLYMPIC STADIUM, MUNICH

Some of the largest stadiums in the world have been built for the Olympic games. The Olympic Stadium in Munich (right) was used for the 1972 Games. It is covered with an enormous glass "tent" roof which is 914,940 sq ft (85,000 sq m) in area – the equivalent of 17 soccer fields. It rests on an enormous steel net that is held up by massive masts.

SKYDOME

The SkyDome (right) in Toronto, Canada, holds the record for the largest retractable roof in the world. In bad weather the roof can be moved to cover the playing area and audience. The seating of the stadium can also be adjusted for different events. It can hold over 50,000 for a baseball game, or 60,000 people for a concert. The SkyDome took just three years to build and was completed in 1989.

THE SKYDOME, TORONTO

WATER WHEEL
The Mohammadieh Noria water wheel (left) in Syria is the biggest water wheel in the world. It is 131 ft (40 m) in diameter and has been in use since Roman times.

Concrete dam

Generators

Turbines

FLOWING WATER has been used as a source of power since the earliest days, from the first water wheels to modern hydroelectric dams. Today, many modern power stations harness the energy of flowing water as a cheap and clean source of electricity.

In most hydroelectric power stations, dams are built to store water. The water from behind the dam is channeled through ducts to turbines that are sent spinning to produce electricity.

THE POWER OF WATER
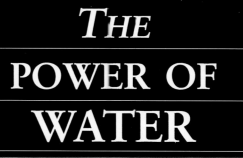

ENORMOUS LAKES
When rivers are dammed, huge areas of land can be flooded to supply the water to generate power. The largest dams can create lakes that cover 3,300 sq miles (8,500 sq km).

Duct opening

DINORWIG

DINORWIG
In a pumped storage station, such as the Dinorwig station in Wales (above), electricity is used to pump water from a lake up to a higher reservoir when demand is low. When there is a sudden demand for power, water flows from the reservoir through tunnels, spinning turbines as it passes to create electricity.

POWER PRODUCTION
Hydroelectric power is now an important source of electricity for many countries around the world. The Itaipu Dam (below) in South America produces enough electricity to supply Brazil with one-quarter of its electricity and neighboring Paraguay with over three-quarters of its demand.

The farther the water falls and the greater the amount that flows through the turbines, the greater the amount of energy produced. To hold back enough water to supply constant electricity, dams tend to be huge structures.

ITAIPU DAM, BRAZIL

INDUSTRIAL GIANTS

*T*he coming of the Industrial Revolution in Europe during the 18th century heralded new types of buildings – large structures devoted solely to manufacturing, mineral extraction, or later, scientific investigation and space exploration. Some of the earliest industrial buildings were ironworks (below). In blast furnaces raw materials were put in the top of the furnace and molten (liquid) iron flowed out of the bottom.

Blast furnace

IRONWORKS

Molten iron

Derrick

PLATFORM

Crane

Drill pipe

Helideck

Supporting legs

Producing wells

OIL RIG
To extract oil from beneath the seabed requires huge oil platforms (right). These oil rigs are self-contained working villages that perch on platforms above the waves. They can be home to more than 100 crew members who live in an accommodation module with canteens, lounges, and meeting rooms. Supporting the rig are huge legs, which can stretch down over 2,640 ft (800 m) to the seabed. The largest rigs can weigh nearly 50,000 tons and produce over 100,000 barrels of oil every day.

OIL REFINERY

With its towers and dense tangle of pipes, a modern oil refinery (right) is an awe-inspiring sight. These refineries convert the crude oil, that is pumped from wells and rigs, into useful products including gasoline. Every refinery has a tall stack with a flare burning from it. This flare is part of the refinery's safety system, where dangerous gases are burned off. The largest refinery in the world is in Venezuela and can process over 530,000 barrels of crude oil a day.

OIL REFINERY

SOLAR POWER

Harnessing energy from the sun to make electricity is pollution-free. In a solar furnace as in Odeillo, France (right), the sun's light is concentrated using mirrors. The heat from this is enough to turn water into steam which drives a turbine and generates electricity.

SOLAR FURNACE, ODEILLO

VEHICLE ASSEMBLY BUILDING

In order to build the huge Saturn V rockets that took astronauts to the Moon, NASA constructed the Vehicle Assembly Building at its site in Florida (below). This massive building is 525 ft (160 m) high, 518 ft (158 m) wide, and 716 ft (218 m) long. The floor area of this huge steel-framed building is 344,352 sq ft (32,000 sq m). Today, the building is used for the assembly of the Space Shuttle.

VEHICLE ASSEMBLY BUILDING

PARTICLE ACCELERATOR

LEP, GENEVA

The huge Large Electron Positron (LEP) collider near Geneva is the world's largest machine. It consists of a huge circular tunnel (above), 17 miles (27 km) in circumference and 12 ft (3.8 m) across. Inside this, particles are accelerated before smashing into other particles. Scientists use this research to find out what atoms are made of.

INSIDE THE LEP TUNNEL

A LOT OF TIME, effort, and money has been invested in creating efficient public transportation systems, such as railroad networks. To reflect the importance of these essential projects many impressive railroad stations have been built around the world. Some of these buildings have to be vast to handle the sheer numbers of people that use them every day. One of the largest is Grand Central Station in New York City.

This huge building covers 2,044,590 sq ft (190,000 sq m) of ground. It was built in 1913, in the heyday of the railroad system in America. Today, over 100 million travelers every year pass through this massive site.

GRAND CENTRAL STATION, NEW YORK

MAIN CONCOURSE

MAIN CONCOURSE
Passengers gather and make their way to their platforms of the Grand Central Station from the huge main concourse (above). The concourse is famous for its extraordinary vaulted ceiling that arches the equivalent of seven stories over the space below. The concourse itself covers some 80,000 sq ft (7,430 sq m) – equivalent to the area of 28 tennis courts.

Subway

WATERLOO TERMINAL

This spectacular station (right) was designed to handle up to 6,000 passengers every hour from the Eurostar trains that link London to Europe via the Channel Tunnel. Opened in 1993, the most striking feature of this 1,312-ft (400-m) long building is its curving roof, with its areas of glass and stainless-steel cladding.

WATERLOO TERMINAL

GRAND CENTRAL STATION

VICTORIA TERMINUS

Now renamed the Mumbai (Bombay) Chhatrapati Sivaji Terminus, the

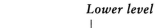

VICTORIA TERMINUS, BOMBAY

Victoria terminus in Bombay (above) is an extravagant building and features many detailed carvings. Some of these near the top of this building, which is 276 ft (84 m) tall, are hard to see from ground level.

Lower level

Main concourse

Traffic ramp

UNDERGROUND

Beneath the main concourse is the heart of Grand Central Station – the tracks themselves. Nearly 34 miles (54 km) of railtrack lie under the station's main building.

COMINGS AND GOINGS

FERRY TERMINUS

A roll-on, roll-off ferry is used when it is convenient to carry a truck and the freight it carries together, rather than unloading the freight into a ship. One of the biggest roll-on, roll-off ports is Dover in England (right), where trucks are loaded onto ships for the short hop across the English Channel. Dover is not only the most important ferry port for the Channel, but is also a main passenger port. The harbor at Dover covers 1 sq mile (2.5 sq km).

DOVER FERRY TERMINUS

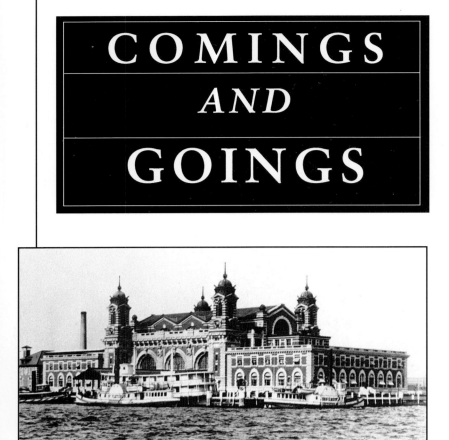

ELLIS ISLAND, NEW YORK

*I*n *a world where travel and trade are vitally important, many huge structures have been put up to allow quick and easy movement of people, cargo, and vehicles. Ellis Island (above), which is 1 mile (1.6 km) to the southwest of the spires of New York City's Manhattan Island, was once the site of the largest immigration station. Between the years 1892 and 1943, when immigration reception to the United States was based in New York, an astonishing 17 million people passed through the island's facilities.*

KANSAI AIRPORT TERMINAL

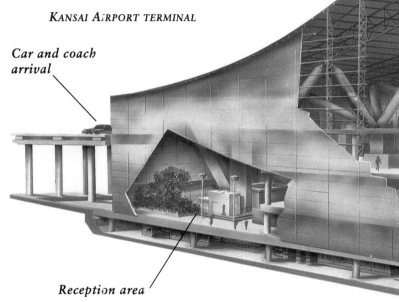

Car and coach arrival

Reception area

ROTTERDAM

The port complex at Rotterdam, Netherlands (left), handles nearly 300 million tons of cargo each year, making it the busiest port in the world.

Much of what the port of Rotterdam itself and its outport, called Europoort, deals with is cargo from the oil industry. To get the largest oil tankers close in to the port, a trench has been dug which is some 16 miles (27 km) long, 4,000 ft (1,220 m) wide, and 74 ft (22 m) deep. It stretches from the port right into the North Sea. The whole port of Rotterdam covers about 38 sq miles (100 sq km) and has over 75 miles (120 km) of quays.

ROTTERDAM DOCKS

KANSAI AIRPORT

Opened in 1994, the massive Kansai Airport is an amazing feat of engineering. The runways and terminals are situated on an artificial island about 3 miles (5 km) off the coast of Japan in Osaka Bay. A six-lane highway as well as rail and high-speed ferry links connect the airport to the mainland. The wing-shaped terminal building (below) stretches for about 1 mile (1.6 km) and is designed to handle nearly 25 million passengers every year.

HEATHROW AIRPORT, 1946

INTERNATIONAL AIRPORTS

When the first commercial airports, such as Heathrow Airport (left) outside London, started just after World War II they were little more than a collection of tents in a field. Since that time airports around the world have grown in size and complexity, many with futuristic buildings, such as the control tower at Los Angeles International Airport (right). Today, Heathrow itself is the world's busiest international airport, handling about 50 million passengers a year.

L.A. INTERNATIONAL AIRPORT

Roof supports

Lattice frame

Machine rooms

Checkpoints

Boarding area

HONG KONG AIRPORT

The new Hong Kong Airport (right), being built at Chek Lap Kok, should be able to handle 50 million passengers every year when it reaches full capacity early in the 21st century. The engineering required exceeds even the construction of Kansai Airport. Two small islands are being leveled and a farther 3 sq miles (9 sq km) of land is being reclaimed from the sea. Its road and rail links to Hong Kong will be 21 miles (34 km) long. These links will include tunnels and the world's longest road-rail suspension bridge.

CHEK LAP KOK, HONG KONG

THE PALACE OF WESTMINSTER

THE KREMLIN

Parts of the Kremlin (right) in Moscow date from the 12th century. Meaning "fortress," the Kremlin is, in fact, a collection of palaces and churches, such as St. Basil's Cathedral. At the Kremlin's center is Red Square, which is 1,320 ft (400 m) by 495 ft (150 m). Nearby there are also government buildings, including the Great Kremlin Palace which has 700 rooms.

THE KREMLIN, MOSCOW

VICTORIA TOWER

At the southwest of the Palace is the Victoria Tower, which at 336 ft (102 m) tall is just slightly taller than St. Stephen's Tower. Over two million documents are stored in the Victoria Tower, including copies of all laws passed since the middle of the 15th century. A Union Jack flag flies from the tower during daylight hours when Parliament is in session.

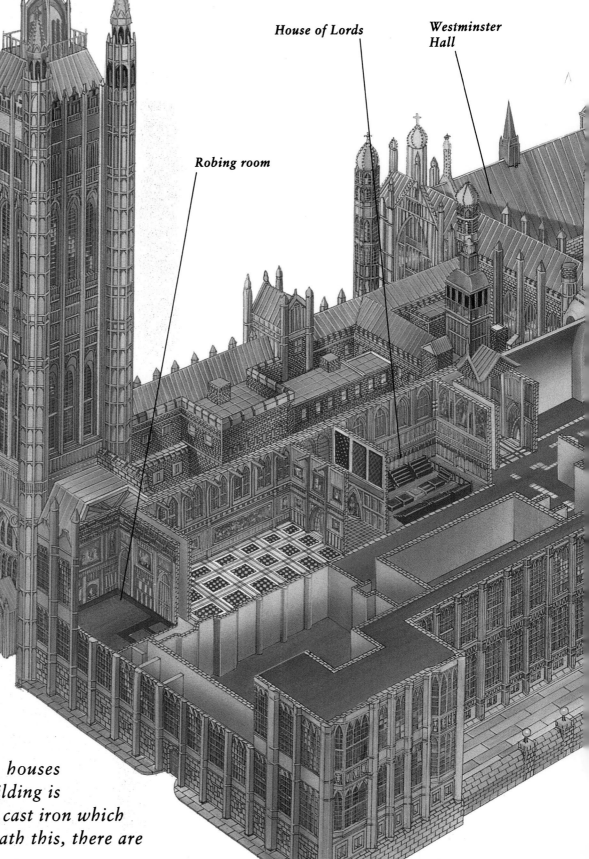

Robing room

House of Lords

Westminster Hall

THE CAPITOL, WASHINGTON D.C.

THE CAPITOL BUILDING

The Capitol Building in Washington, D.C. (above), houses the U.S. Congress. The building is topped by a dome made of cast iron which is 287 ft (87 m) high. Beneath this, there are some 540 rooms.

ST. STEPHEN'S TOWER

At the eastern end of the Palace of Westminster sits St. Stephen's Tower. It is 330 ft (100 m) tall and holds the 13-ton bell known as Big Ben. The four faces of the clock are 23 ft (7 m) across and have numerals that are 2 ft (0.6 m) tall. A light shines from the tower when Parliament is sitting at night.

House of Commons

Tea terrace

GOVERNMENT BUILDINGS tend to be impressive places to reflect their important role in society. One of the most beautiful and ornate is the Palace of Westminster in London. Although the main buildings of the Palace were put up in the middle of the 19th century, they were built using the Gothic style of the medieval period. The Palace has 2 miles (3 km) of corridors and 1,100 rooms, including both the House of Commons and the House of Lords, as well as offices for Members of Parliament, several restaurants and bars, a gymnasium, and even a shooting range.

INSIDE THE CHAMBERS

The two debating chambers of the Houses of Parliament are the House of Commons, where the 659 Members of Parliament sit, and the House of Lords. The floor of the House of Commons is divided in two so that the governing body faces the opposition. They are separated by two lines that have been drawn two sword lengths apart. This was done to prevent Members from attacking each other.

THE PALACE OF WESTMINSTER, LONDON

PUBLIC BUILDINGS

L ike government offices, public
buildings have many other roles. These
include being banks, museums, and
even prisons. The huge Pentagon building
(below) in Arlington County, Virginia, near
Washington, D.C., is home to the U.S.
Department of Defense. When it was
completed in 1943, it was the largest office
building in the world. The Pentagon has over
17 miles (28 km) of corridors, its own
shopping area, a bus station, parking for
10,000 cars, and its own heliport.

BANK OF ENGLAND

THE BANK OF ENGLAND

The Bank of England
earned its nickname
"The Old Lady of
Threadneedle Street"
when it moved into
Threadneedle Street in
London in 1734. The
present-day structure
was completed in 1828
after considerable
rebuilding under the
supervision of the architect Sir
John Soane. Today, the bank covers 130,000
sq ft (12,000 sq m). Throughout its history
the building has housed the central bank of
the United Kingdom. This has been
responsible for raising money for wars,
for issuing bank notes, and for setting
interest rates.

ALCATRAZ

Also known as "The Rock,"
Alcatraz Island (below) is found
some 1.5 miles (2 km) off the
coast in San Francisco Bay. It
was a prison between 1934 and
1963 and contained some of
America's most dangerous
prisoners. The rocky island's
prison buildings had space for 450
convicts in cells, but only about 250 were
ever housed there at any one time. Infamous
criminals such as Al Capone and George "Machine Gun"
Kelly spent time in Alcatraz.

THE PENTAGON, VIRGINIA

ALCATRAZ

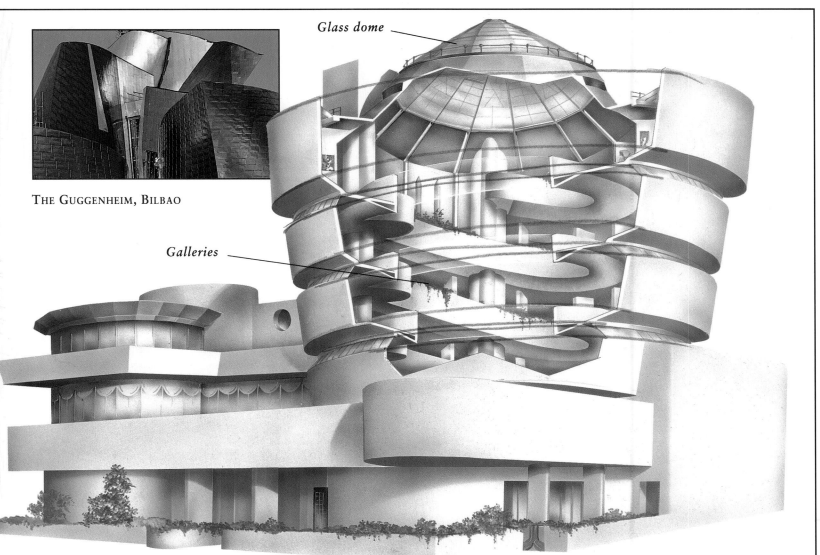

Glass dome

Galleries

THE GUGGENHEIM, BILBAO

LOUVRE

Formerly the site of the French Royal Court, the Louvre was opened as a public museum in 1793 after the French Revolution. Since then the museum has been added to consistently, and today there are over 8 miles (13 km) of galleries. These galleries house many famous works of art, including the Mona Lisa (also known as La Gioconda). Expansion continues today, and in 1989 a glass pyramid was built over the entrance to the museum (below).

THE GUGGENHEIM MUSEUMS

The Guggenheim Museum in New York City (above), completed in 1959, contains a collection of modern paintings. American architect Frank Lloyd Wright designed the building so that visitors could take an elevator to the top and then walk along a ramp that spirals down to the first floor. A similarly unconventional Guggenheim Museum building is being completed in Bilbao (top), Spain. The building, designed by Frank O'Gehry, is topped by a gleaming metal roof.

THE BRITISH LIBRARY

THE BRITISH LIBRARY

The new British Library building in London (right) covers over 323,000 sq ft (30,000 sq m) and has nearly 213 miles (340 km) of shelving. Most of the shelves, nearly 150 miles (240 km), are held in the vast basement area, which covers four levels. Altogether, a total of nearly 150 million items, including 12 million books, are stored in this vast library.

THE LOUVRE, PARIS

REACH FOR THE SKY

HEAD IN THE CLOUDS

Working hundreds of feet above the ground is dangerous at the best of times. However, in the early days of skyscraper building, workers would clamber over the steel frame of the building without hard hats or safety harnesses and with little regard for the dangers of falling from a height (left).

CONSTRUCTION WORKER ON THE EMPIRE STATE

W here both land prices and the demand for housing are high, the only way to build is up. The first skyscraper is widely recognized as having been the Home Insurance Company Building, built in the business district of Chicago in 1885. Although it was only ten stories high, it was nevertheless a giant of its time. The building owed its height to a strong framework of iron girders that supported the building's entire weight. Once

builders found they could reach new heights, structures started shooting into the sky. The first half of the 20th century saw the height of the tallest building soar from about 300 ft (90 m) to 1,250 ft (381 m). This period also saw the development of many innovations that were important for the development of the skyscraper. These included high speed elevators to carry people quickly and easily up the many floors of a skyscraper and air-conditioning to maintain the temperature.

THE EMPIRE STATE BUILDING

When it was completed in 1931, the Empire State Building became the tallest building in the world and held that record for over 40 years. Today, nearly 15,000 people work in the building for 850 companies. To get to the top of the building people can choose to use any of the 73 elevators that travel up and down 7 miles (11 km) of elevator shafts, or they could walk up the breathtaking 1,860 steps!

The Flatiron Building, New York 285 ft (87 m)

The Woolworth Building, New York 793 ft (241 m)

The Chrysler Building, New York 1,046 ft (319 m)

The Empire State Building, New York 1,250 ft (381 m)

The Pyramid of Cheops, Giza 451 ft (138 m)

LATE 20TH CENTURY TOWERS

The erection of the Empire State Building marked a limit in skyscraper construction. With the technology of the day, taller buildings would have been too heavy to build and too weak to cope with the stresses involved, including swaying caused by high winds. Since that time, improvements in design and materials used in construction have pushed the height of buildings higher with structures such as the World Trade Center in New York, and the Petronas Towers in Malaysia (below).

MILLENNIUM TOWER, TOKYO

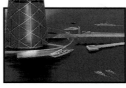

When it is completed, the proposed Millennium Tower in Tokyo (left) will be 2,500 ft (762 m) high – almost twice the height of the Sears Tower. Its cone shape will help reduce wind forces, and the use of a lightweight frame will reduce stress on the tower. The Millennium Tower will be like a city in the sky, containing lodging, shops, movie theaters, food courts, and even gardens.

The World Trade Center, New York
1,368 ft (417 m)

The Sears Tower, Chicago
1,454 ft (443 m)

The Petronas Towers, Malaysia
1,476 ft (450 m)

JUST NORTH OF THE Mexican border are the enormous greenhouse buildings of Biosphere II. This futuristic structure is a test site to see how different environments react in a sealed system and also how well humans might survive on long space missions to other planets. Inside the massive, sealed greenhouse a number of different environments have been created that are totally cut off from the outside world. Twice, a group of men and women were sealed in for a long period of time to see if they could manage an artificial world containing several thousand species of plants and animals.

BIOSPHERE II

BREATHING BUILDING

To stop the pressure inside Biosphere II from cracking the building when the air expands as it is heated up each day by the sun, the designers built a special "lung" device. This expands and contracts to even out the pressure inside Biosphere II as the temperature varies.

"Lung"

Intensive Agriculture Biome

Glass structure

AROUND THE SITE

Biosphere II covers 130,000 sq ft (12,000 sq m) of the Arizona desert. Its buildings are 91 ft (28 m) tall and are made up of 16,000 panes of glass, which create an airtight environment and seal the contents completely. Underneath the building sits a 500-ton stainless-steel plate. This prevents anything from getting into the building from below that might "contaminate" the experiment's results.

BIOSPHERE II

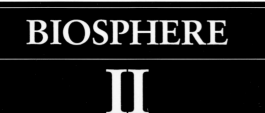

INSIDE BIOSPHERE II

Behind the glass structure are living quarters for the humans, as well as several different types of environments, or biomes. The Intensive Agriculture Biome supplied the inhabitants with their food. The other biomes are rainforest, thornscrub, savannah, desert, marsh, and ocean.

DIFFERENT BIOMES INSIDE BIOSPHERE II

Human accommodation

Rainforest biome

Savannah biome

Ocean biome

Thornscrub biome

Marsh biome

Desert biome

OCEAN BIOME

LIVING EXPERIMENT

Two groups of humans were sealed inside Biosphere II, the first group for two years begining in 1991, the second for almost seven months in 1994. They monitored the different environments and grew the food they needed to survive. During the two experiments they noticed that nearly a third of the animals and plant species died.

THE
TOMIGAYA II
BUILDING

BUILDING
THE
FUTURE

THE GREEN BUILDING

*A*rchitects and builders of the future will have to cope with many different problems. Space will be at a premium and answers will be needed to solve the world's housing crisis. Buildings themselves will also have to be more efficient, conserving the planet's dwindling natural resources. The Tomigaya II building (right), to be constructed in Tokyo, is designed to be self-sufficient in energy. The shape of the building increases wind speed around the structure, allowing a wind turbine to supply power. The three-legged Green Building (above) ventilates itself by drawing in fresh air from beneath the main building and pushing out stale air through the roof.

BUILDING IN SPACE

One solution to the shortage of land would be to leave the planet altogether. Orbiting space stations, like the Russian Mir, have been occupied since the 1960s and the International Space Station (left) will provide a permanently inhabited station that could become a jumping-off point for missions to other planets. Many companies have also put forward ideas for permanent bases on other planets, including the Moon and Mars.

INTERNATIONAL SPACE STATION

FLOATING CITIES

Many of today's cities lie on the coast where there is little room to expand. One solution would be to reclaim land from the sea or even create a floating city (above). Reclaimed land could also provide wide-open spaces of park land that may no longer exist in older cities.

WORLD BENEATH YOUR FEET

As well as building up to solve the problem of space, architects have also looked to the ground beneath our feet. An underground city (above) would be shielded from variations in weather and could even create its own climate. Air from the outside could be filtered and cleaned to provide the inhabitants with a pollution-free environment.

UP, UP, AND AWAY

Many corporations have put forward plans for buildings that would dwarf even the proposed Millennium Tower (see page 33). One of these, the X-Seed 4000 (right) designed by the Taisei Construction Company, would stretch over 2.5 miles (4 km) into the sky.

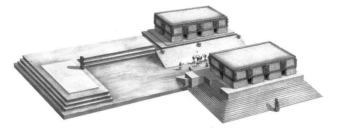

GLOSSARY

Amphitheater
A building with rows of seats surrounding an oval-shaped open space, called the arena. In the arena, games and competitions, including battles and gladiator fights, were held in Roman times.

Aqueduct
An artificial channel or pipe that carries a large amount of water, often across a valley on top of a bridge.

Barracks
A building or a group of buildings used to house soldiers.

Basilica
A type of religious building which usually consists of a rectangular hall that has a semi-circular recess at one end.

Buttresses
Projecting supports built onto the outside of a wall. A flying buttress is an outside support built into the shape of an arch.

Cathedral
The principal xChristian church in an area, or diocese. Cathedrals contain the bishop's throne, called a cathedra.

Cladding
The outer "skin" covering the walls of a building.

Crypt
An underground chamber of a church that often holds graves.

Dam
A wall or bank that is used to hold back water. Dams can be made from concrete or earth. Many have turbines through which water flows to produce electricity.

Dome
A hemispherical (half-ball-shaped) structure that is found on top of a building.

Foundations
The base of a building, which is usually sunk into the ground and which stops the building from sinking.

Gothic
An architectural style, dating from the 12th to the 16th centuries. The style was typified by high-pointed arches and ornate decorations.

Keep
The stone or wooden tower that forms the defensive heart of a castle.

Masonry
The stonework of a building.

Mosque
A Muslim place of worship. Most mosques have between one and six towers, called minarets, from which the muezzins (criers) call people to prayer.

Nave
The main part of a church, usually found to the west of the center of the "cross" made by the church's outline.

Pyramid
A five-sided shape with a square base and four triangular sides. Many cultures, including the ancient Egyptians, used this shape as the basis for some of their buildings.

Skyscraper
A very tall, multi-story building.

Temple
A building or place of worship that is dedicated to, or regarded as, the house of a god.

Transept
A wing, or part of a church found at right angles to the nave.

CHRONOLOGY

2650 B.C. The first great Egyptian pyramid is built for King Zoser, who lived between 2668 and 2649 B.C.

2580 B.C. The Great Pyramid of Cheops is completed and becomes the world's tallest building for 4,000 years.

300 B.C. The Chinese begin construction of the Great Wall of China. It still remains the largest object created by humans.

A.D. 82 The Colosseum in Rome is completed by the Emperor Domitian.

A.D. 532 The Emperor Justinian begins construction of Hagia Sophia in Constantinople (Istanbul).

1142 Crusader knights move into Krak des Chevaliers, Syria.

1238 Moorish princes start to build the Alhambra Palace in southern Spain.

1271 Sultan Beibars tricks the occupiers of Krak des Chevaliers into surrendering.

1358 The Alhambra Palace is completed.

1453 Constantinople falls to the Ottoman Turks and Hagia Sophia is converted into a mosque.

1526 King Charles V of Spain has many parts of the Alhambra Palace rebuilt.

1609 The Japanese warlord, Ikeda Teramusa, expands Himeji Castle in Japan.

1631 The Emperor Shah Jahan begins to build the Taj Mahal mausoleum to hold the body of his dead wife.

1654 The Taj Mahal is completed.

1660 Work begins on building the Palace of Versailles and continues for another 100 years.

1710 St. Paul's Cathedral in London is completed.

1850 French missionary, Father Charles-Emile Bouillevaus, stumbles across the remains of the ancient city of Angkor in the Cambodian Jungle.

1862 Building starts on the Paris Opéra, designed by Charles Garnier.

1869 Ludwig II of Bavaria begins construction of his fantastic Neuschwanstein Castle on a rocky crag.

1870 The new Palace of Westminster is completed after the old palace was destroyed by fire in 1834.

1885 The ten-story Home Insurance Building is completed in Chicago, making it the world's first skyscraper.

1886 Having been completed in Paris the previous year, the Statue of Liberty is shipped to New York and erected on its present site.

1889 The Eiffel Tower is completed in Paris.

1913 The Woolworth Building is completed in New York, becoming the world's tallest building.

1930 The Chrysler Building is completed in New York.

1931 The Empire State Building in New York is completed, becoming the world's tallest building.

1934 Hagia Sophia is stripped of religious significance and turned into a museum.

1936 The Crystal Palace in London is destroyed by fire.

1959 The Guggenheim Museum in New York is completed.

1972 The twin towers of the World Trade Center in New York are completed.

1973 The Sydney Opera House is opened.

1974 Building work ends on the Sears Tower in Chicago. It took four years to build and succeeds the World Trade Center as the world's tallest building.

1989 The SkyDome in Toronto, home of the Toronto Blue Jays baseball team, is completed.

1991 Eight people are sealed inside Biosphere II, and remain there for two years.

1997 The Petronas Towers in Kuala Lumpur, Malaysia, are completed, becoming the world's tallest building.

INDEX

Photographic credits:

Abbreviations: t-top, m-middle, b-bottom, r-right, l-left

Pages 4b, 7bl & bm, 8tl, 10tr, 11bl, 14m, 15tr, 17, 19br, 21b, 22bl & bm, 24b, 26tl & tr, 27b, 30t & m, 31t & bl, 32m, 34, 35tm & tr & 37 all – Frank Spooner Pictures. 5t – Novosti Picture Library. 5b, 6t, 8tr, 9, 10b, 11m & br, 13t, 14tl, 19bl, 20, 22m, 24t, 25tr, 26b, 27m, 28 both & 29 – Spectrum Colour Library. 6m & b, 16, 18t & 32t – Mary Evans Picture Library. 7br, 15tl & 25tl – Eye Ubiquitous. 10tl & m – Flick Killerby. 13b, 14tr & b, 19m & 22br – James Davis Travel Photography. 21t – CEGB. 22t – Solution Pictures. 27t – Adrian Meredith Photography. 31br – Paul Nightingale. 35tl & b – Science Photo Library. 36b & Back Cover – NASA.